CHRIST IS COME

A CANDLELIGHT CELEBRATION
FOR ADVENT AND CHRISTMAS EVE

SHARONN DAVIS HALDERMAN

CHRIST IS COME!

9045 / ISBN 1-55673-257-0

Dedicated to the congregation of St. Paul's United Methodist Church in Red Lion, Pennsylvania, who nourished me and taught me many things.

The Service

These five services were originally conceived as separate presentations to be incorporated into regularly scheduled Advent and Christmas Eve celebrations. You will find that when used in this way, your congregation will anticipate the excitement of new insights each week, while enjoying the familiarity of your traditional order of worship.

Alternately, the services may be combined as a single Christmas Eve celebration recalling the anticipation of Advent and its fulfillment at Christmas with the birth of the Christ child. You will find a complete Order of Worship for this purpose following the individual presentations in this book.

Advent 1

COVENANT

Scripture Reading: *The Lord says, "The time is coming when I will make a new covenant with the people of Israel and with the people of Judah . . . The new covenant that I will make with the people of Israel will be this: I will put my law within them and write it on their hearts. I will be their God, and they will be my people.* (Jeremiah 31:31, 33 GNFMM)

(Light the first candle on the Advent Wreath.)

Reflection:
It is time to light the first candle on the Advent Wreath — the Covenant Candle. A covenant is a promise or a binding agreement. The covenant relationship between God and people played an important part in the history of our faith. God made a covenant with Abraham — with Moses — with the Hebrew People. God demanded faithfulness and promised blessings.

The Old Testament recounts the continual failure of the people to be faithful to their promises. The future of the Covenant Community seemed doomed to failure. Then

God inspired the prophet Jeremiah to bring this message: *"Behold the days are coming when I will make a New Covenant."* The new covenant was unique in that it would be written upon the hearts of the people, and not upon tablets of stone.

A new covenant? A ray of light to shine in the midst of dark despair? But, when would the new covenant be made? How? Surely, God's promise could not be revealed in a stable amid animal smells and noises! Certainly, a humble peasant girl could not be included in a Divine Drama. Most assuredly, God's new covenant could not be connected with the birth of a child. And yet . . . and yet . . . how indelibly that humble event is etched into our imaginations and written upon our hearts!

Today there is despair and darkness in our world. There is a lack of trust and a sense of failure. During Advent, we again wait with expectation to receive Christ — the One who will deliver us. We feel a new sense of hope as we await the continual unfolding of God's plan.

Prayer: *Dear God, Thank you for being faithful to your Covenant with us. Forgive us, for we, like the Hebrews of old, have broken our Covenant with you. We await the fulfillment of your promises to us. Help us open our lives to You and one another as we prepare to receive the New Covenant. Amen*

Hymn: "O Come, O Come, Emmanuel" *(v. 1)*

Advent 2

ORDINARY

Scripture Reading: *There were some shepherds . . . in the fields, taking care of their flocks. An angel of the Lord appeared to them, and the glory of the Lord shone over them. They were terribly afraid, but the angel said to them, "Don't be afraid! I am here with good news for you which will bring great joy to all the people.* (Luke 2:8-10 GNFMM)

(Light the second candle on the Advent Wreath.)

Reflection:

Advent is a time of preparation — a time of waiting and preparing for the Lord to come. The first Advent candle and the letter **C** called to mind our **C**ovenant relationship with God. Now, we light the second Advent candle and think of the letter **O** which reminds us of the **O**rdinary. Humans seem to be attracted by the spectacular — unimpressed by the ordinary.

However, the Scriptures reveal that God often chooses to make Divine revelations through the everyday — the commonplace — the ordinary. The Old Testament prophets

8

communicated God's promise to send a Deliverer to the people of Israel. The people expected that the Promised One would be as popular as David — as wise as Solomon — mighty and powerful — able to destroy all Israel's enemies, and that the coming of the Promised One would bring about a general sense of peace and prosperity.

There was no room in this grand vision for a tiny helpless infant, sleeping in a manger. Significantly, it was to the shepherds — busy at their daily work — that the news of the birth of the promised Savior was revealed. In response to the announcement, the shepherds hurried to Bethlehem to see the tiny baby that had been overlooked by the bustling, noisy crowds.

Today, we place much emphasis upon the strong — the scientific — the intellectual. Too often we ignore or disdain the ordinary. Is it possible that in our frantic self-seeking we, too, have failed to be aware of Christ in our midst? This year let us be aware of the Holy in small quiet acts of kindness and loving concern. Let us consciously prepare a place for Christ in our everyday, commonplace, ordinary lives.

Prayer: *God of Love, Thank you for sending Christ to us at Christmas. Help us to recognize you in ordinary symbols like the cup, the bread, the water, and human relationships. Amen*

Hymn: "O Come, O Come, Emmanuel" *(v. 2)*

Advent 3

MESSAGE

Scripture Reading: *Don't be afraid! I am here with good news for you, which will bring great joy to all the people. This very day in David's town your Savior was born — Christ the Lord! And this is what will prove it to you: you will find a baby wrapped in cloths and lying in a manger.* (Luke 2:10b-12 GNFMM)

(Light the third candle on the Advent Wreath.)

Reflection:

Traditionally, the third Advent candle is the Joy Candle. At this time, we light the pink candle and ponder the **Message** of joy that comes to us in this season.

In December it is customary to send greetings to family and friends. As we address cards and lick stamps it is appropriate to recall a unique message that was sung by angels long ago: *"Fear not, for, behold, I bring you good tidings of great joy, which shall be to all people. For unto you is born this day in the city of David a Saviour, which is Christ the Lord."*

10

God's Messengers did not use colorful pictures and lyrical verses to greet the people of the earth. Instead, they brought "good tidings of great joy." They brought a Message of prophecy fulfilled — a Message of future possibilities. And, as the angels' song faded away, hope was born in the hearts of those who heard and received the message. The hope was for peace, forgiveness, and reconciliation.

That timeless message comes to us again this Advent season. We try to capture the message, explain it, and act it out in many ways — through the use of songs and carols, decorations, sermons, and pageants. Whether our explanations succeed or fail is not of major importance. The important thing is that we acknowledge and receive anew God's joyous, hopeful Message of love that came down at Christmas.

Prayer: *Dear God, Thank you for the song of God's special Messengers, the angels. May we listen to the joyful song and respond in faith to their hopeful message. May our daily lives reflect the hope that message brings to our hearts today. Amen*

Hymn: "O Come, O Come, Emmanuel" *(v. 3)*

Advent 4

EXPECTATIONS

Scripture Reading: *When he came near Jerusalem at the place where the road went down the Mount of Olives, the large crowd of his disciples began to thank God and praise him in loud voices for all the great things they had seen: "God bless the king who comes in the name of the Lord! Peace in heaven and glory to God!"* (Luke 19:37-38 GNFMM)

(Light the fourth candle on the Advent Wreath.)

Reflection:

During Advent and Christmas the level of Expectation is high. Perhaps we are anticipating joyous family get-togethers, delicious meals, the perfect gift, meaningful worship services, or pleasant feelings of peace and good will toward others. But, how often does the reality of our human experience fall short of our expectations? How often do we experience the "after-Christmas-blues" because our December 25 expectations have not been met, and we feel let down and disappointed?

12

The people of Palestine also had high expectations as they awaited the coming of a Divine Deliverer. They dreamed of a tall, strong, lusty king who would ride on a splendid beast. This conqueror would sweep across the land, lift the burdens from the people, and defeat all their enemies. In addition, this Messiah would be loved and adored by all. It was a grand vision, but a fanciful expectation.

God — in Infinite wisdom — did send a Deliverer, but in an unexpected way. Jesus came as a tiny, helpless, newborn child, and was laid in a manger where animals ate. The birth went unheralded by the mighty and powerful, but was celebrated by angels and hard-working shepherds. When Jesus grew up, he walked through the land, talking with individuals and helping them to find inner strength in order to deal with their problems. Jesus was loved by some, hated and feared by many. At last, his enemies crucified him. Crucifixion was not the end, but the beginning. It was a necessary part of God's plan to defeat our most feared enemy — death.

As we wait expectantly during Advent and Christmas, let us look deeply into the remains of wrinkled wrapping paper and crushed bows that symbolize our disappointments, and find there the memory of a small child who grew up to fulfill our Expectations by making it possible for us to receive the gift of Eternal Life.

Prayer: *God of all Knowledge, Help us to have realistic expectations and to make necessary preparations for our spiritual growth. May we increase our awareness of the responsibilities of discipleship. Inspire us to affirm our Christian faith as we live each day faithfully. Amen*

Hymn: "O Come, O Come, Emmanuel" *(v. 4)*

Christmas Eve

CHRIST IS COME!

Scripture Reading: *So they hurried off and found Mary and Joseph and saw the baby lying in the manger. When the shepherds saw him, they told them what the angel had said about the child. All who heard it were amazed at what the shepherds said. Mary remembered all these things and thought deeply about them.* (Luke 2:16-19 GNFMM)

(Light the Christ Candle.)

Reflection:

Finally tonight we light the Christ Candle and triumphantly proclaim that **Christ Is Come!** Christ is Emmanuel — God with us!

The waiting is ended! Our prayers are answered. A light shines into the darkness of our world and our lives!

Christ is come to renew the **C**ovenant relationship with us. Christ is come into the **O**rdinary and unexpected places of our lives. Christ is come to bring a **M**essage of love, forgiveness, and reconciliation. Christ is come as a fulfillment of the age-old **E**xpectations regarding One who would deliver the people from their sins.

14

We gaze at the tiny baby nestled amid the winking colored lights of our nativity scenes, and we feel a surge of joy. Most of us realize that the beauty and warmth of our depictions of the nativity are far removed from the cold discomfort of the smelly, noisy stable in which Christ was born. We take pleasure in the comfortable, and such a thought disturbs us. But, Christ came to disturb us, to challenge us, to inspire us to seek a better way, a higher path, a more meaningful life. Tonight, we remember with gratitude Christ's life, ministry, and ultimate death as a sacrifice for our sins.

On this quiet, holy night we joyfully celebrate the anniversary of Christ's coming into our world. We thrill again at the angels' song: *"Fear not, for behold I bring you good tidings of great joy, which shall be to all people. For unto you is born this day in the city of David a Saviour, which is Christ the Lord. And this shall be a sign unto you; Ye shall find the babe wrapped in swaddling cloths, lying in a manger."*

Christ Is Come! God is here with us! Let us Rejoice and be glad!

Prayer: *God of Life, Thank you for the gift of Jesus Christ, our Savior. Thank you for sending Christ to be born and to live among us. Thank you for Christ's example of life perfectly lived. Inspire us to seek to imitate Christ in our lives. Amen.*

Hymn: "Joy to the World"

An Order of Worship for Christmas Eve

Scripture Reading   *Jeremiah 31:31, 33*

Lighting of the First Candle / Presentation of Letter **C**

Reflection   **Covenant**

Prayer

Hymn   *"O Come, O Come, Emmanuel" (v. 1)*

Scripture Reading   *Luke 2:8-10*

Lighting of the Second Candle / Presentation of Letter **O**

Reflection   **Ordinary**

Prayer

Hymn   *"O Come, O Come, Emmanuel" (v. 2)*

Scripture Reading   *Luke 2:10b-12*

Lighting of the Third Candle / Presentation of Letter **M**

Reflection   **Message**

Prayer

Hymn   *"O Come, O Come, Emmanuel" (v. 3)*

Scripture Reading   *Luke 19:37-38*

Lighting of the Fourth Candle / Presentation of Letter **E**

Reflection   **Expectations**

Prayer

Hymn   *"O Come, O Come, Emmanuel" (v. 4)*

Scripture Reading   *Luke 2:16-19*

Lighting of the Christ Candle / Completion of Banner

Reflection   Christ Is Come!

Prayer

Hymn   *"Joy to the World"*

The Banner

The mood of Advent is one of Expectation. To enhance this mood and give the congregation something special to anticipate, prepare a Banner to which something is added on each of the four Sundays of Advent and on Christmas Eve.

Dimensions of the Banner: L - 44" x W - 36"

Color of the Banner: Lavender or White

Letters are added prior to each Sunday's Worship Celebration during Advent, and the color of each letter corresponds to the color of the Advent Candle lighted during the service. The order would be as follows:

Advent 1 — **C** — purple or violet
Advent 2 — **O** — purple or violet
Advent 3 — **M** — pink
Advent 4 — **E** — purple or violet

(**Note:** If you use a different color pattern for your Advent wreath — substitute the appropriate colors.)

The letters are placed diagonally, reading down from the top left corner to the bottom right corner of the banner. If you choose to use this material as a single service for Christmas Eve, it would be most effective to allow younger members of your congregation to present the letters and other elements of the Banner before each Reflection, either before or after each candle is lit. You will find that attaching Velcro to the pieces beforehand will make your transitions smooth and certain. On Christmas Eve the words **Christ Is** are added to the upper right hand corner of the Banner, and the Nativity Symbol is added to the lower left hand corner of the Banner. Colors for **Christ Is** and the Nativity Symbol are optional. Some padding behind the portion of the symbol representing the child is very effective.

Scale: 1 square = 4 inches

www.ingramcontent.com/pod-product-compliance
Lightning Source LLC
Chambersburg PA
CBHW060045040426
42331CB00032B/2479